Ferris Wheels

by Grace Hansen

Abdo Kids Jumbo is an Imprint of Abdo Kids
abdopublishing.com

abdopublishing.com

Published by Abdo Kids, a division of ABDO, P.O. Box 398166, Minneapolis, Minnesota 55439.
Copyright © 2019 by Abdo Consulting Group, Inc. International copyrights reserved in all countries.
No part of this book may be reproduced in any form without written permission from the publisher.
Abdo Kids Jumbo™ is a trademark and logo of Abdo Kids.

052018
092018

 THIS BOOK CONTAINS
RECYCLED MATERIALS

Photo Credits: Alamy, Getty Images, Granger Collection, iStock, Shutterstock

Production Contributors: Teddy Borth, Jennie Forsberg, Grace Hansen

Design Contributors: Dorothy Toth, Laura Mitchell

Library of Congress Control Number: 2017960576

Publisher's Cataloging-in-Publication Data

Names: Hansen, Grace, author.

Title: Ferris wheels / by Grace Hansen.

Description: Minneapolis, Minnesota : Abdo Kids, 2019. | Series: Amusement park rides |
    Includes glossary, index and online resources (page 24).

Identifiers: ISBN 9781532108013 (lib.bdg.) | ISBN 9781532108990 (ebook) |
    ISBN 9781532109485 (Read-to-me ebook)

Subjects: LCSH: Ferris wheels--Juvenile literature. | Amusement rides--Juvenile literature. |
    Amusement parks--Juvenile literature.

Classification: DDC 791.068--dc23

Table of Contents

The First Great Wheels

Rides like Ferris wheels appeared in the early 1600s. They were very different from the giant wheels we see today.

In 1620, Peter Mundy visited what is now Bulgaria. He watched a large man turn a vertical wheel. The wheel had chairs attached to it. Riders were happy to be on it!

Rides similar to the one
Mundy saw began to appear
throughout Europe and Asia.

The ride first came to America in 1848. It helped attract people to a fair in Georgia. Today, Ferris wheels can be found at almost every fair.

Somers' Roundabout

In 1893 William Somers
patented the Roundabout.
It was made of wood. A man
named George Ferris Jr. rode it.

W. SOMERS.
ROUNDABOUT.
No. 489,238.   Patented Jan. 3, 1893.

Fig. 2.

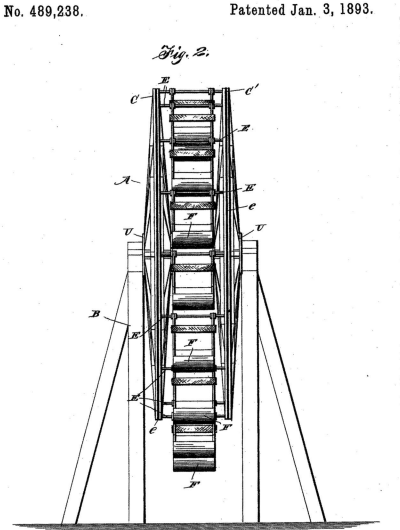

Inventor
William Somers
by E.W. Anderson
his Attorney

W. SOMERS.
ROUNDABOUT.
No. 489,238.   Patented Jan. 3, 1893.

Fig. 1.

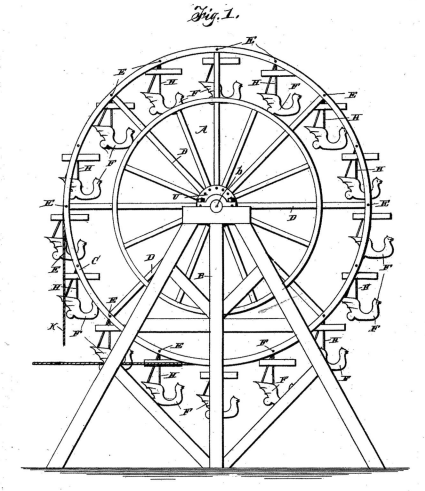

Inventor
William Somers
by E.W. Anderson
his Attorney

13

The Ferris Wheel

The 1893 **world's fair** was held in Chicago. Ferris Jr. built a 264-foot (80.5 m), steel wheel for it. He called it a Ferris wheel.

George Ferris Jr.

The wheel turned on a 45.5-foot (14 m) steel **axle**. It had 36 cars. Each car carried up to 60 people. More than 38,000 people rode it each day!

17

Today there are many Ferris wheels, large and small. The High Roller is in Las Vegas. It was built in 2014. It is 550 feet (167.6 m) tall!

19

The Ain Dubai in Dubai

was completed in 2018.

It is an amazing 668 feet

(203.6 m) tall! It can carry

1,400 passengers at once.

More Facts

- The **axle** for Ferris's first wheel was the largest piece of steel ever **forged**.

- Before the Ferris wheel, the ride went by many names: Ups-and-downs, pleasure wheels, Roundabouts, big wheels, great wheels, and more.

- The **world's fair** of 1893 had to compete with the 1889 world's fair, which amazed visitors with the Eiffel Tower.

Glossary

axle – a bar or shaft on which a wheel turns.

forge – to form or shape by heating and hammering.

patent – a government grant that gives someone the right to make, use, or sell an invention.

world's fair – an international exhibition that showcases the industrial, scientific, technological, and artistic creations of the participating nations.

Index

Abdo Kids ONLINE
FREE! ONLINE MULTIMEDIA RESOURCES

Visit **abdokids.com** and use this code to access crafts, games, videos, and more!

Abdo Kids Code:
AFK8013